Each Broken Object

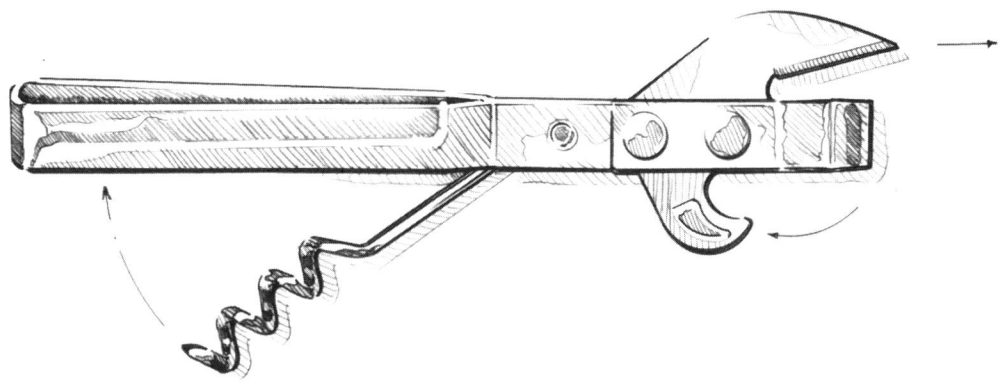

David Greenslade

Published in Great Britain, 2000
By Two Rivers Press
35-39 London Street
Reading, Berkshire RG1 4PS
United Kingdom

© poems David Greenslade
© illustrations Andy Penaluna

ISBN 1-901677-230

Design Jim Noble

Printed and bound in the UK by Antony Rowe Ltd,
Bumper's Farm, Chippenham, Wiltshire

Thanks to the editors of the following magazines:
Angel Exhaust, Apostrophe, Bound Spiral, Cencrastus, First Offence, First Time, Oasis, Obsessed with Pipework, Poets Artists & Madmen (USA), News That Stays News, Poetry Wales, SwagMag, Swansea Review, Terrible Work, Things Journal; Unruly Sun. Lace is a tribute poem in memory of Eva Loewe, founder of The New Lacemakers. Objects Return in Triumph from their Exile previously appeared in Welsh and Catalan in the publication Pebyll; Kayak first appeared in the Gwasg Israddol pamphlet Old Emulsion Customs; Hi-Fi appears courtesy of First Pressings, Faber & Faber. Clogs first appeared as Sabot Guido Gezelle (internet poetry project, Brugge).

Contents

Paperclip	*page 5*
Railway	*page 6*
The Object's Side	*page 7*
First Job	*page 8*
Bicycle Spanner	*page 10*
Mandrel	*page 11*
Glove	*page 12*
Oxygen Cylinder	*page 12*
Cardboard Box	*page 13*
Pencil Sharpener	*page 14*
Coat Hanger	*page 15*
Washers	*page 16*
Watering Can	*page 17*
Tin Opener	*page 18*
Net	*page 20*
I Came Upon Their Camp	*page 21*
Briefcase	*page 22*
Barrow	*page 23*
Her Things	*page 24*
Wedge	*page 25*
Lace	*page 26*
Latch	*page 27*
Ball Pien Hammer	*page 28*
Bucket	*page 28*
Going to Meet	*page 29*
Toothpaste Tube	*page 30*
Primordial Browsers	*page 32*
Combination Eyeglasses/Eggslicer	*page 34*
Leaflets	*page 35*
Petrol Nozzle	*page 36*
Kerb	*page 37*
Hi-Fi	*page 38*
Tables and Elbows	*page 40*
Soup Bowl	*page 41*
Kayaks	*page 42*
Soap Seller	*page 43*
Belt &	*page 44*
Home Plumbing Catalogue	*page 45*
Sellotape	*page 46*
Sweeping Brush	*page 47*
Wired Glass	*page 48*
Wire	*page 48*
Roller-Blade	*page 49*
Walls Filled With Fat	*page 50*
Bier	*page 51*
Tumour	*page 52*
Key	*page 54*
Rivet	*page 55*
Raffle Ticket	*page 56*
Plastic Bag	*page 57*
Ladder	*page 58*
Objects Return in Triumph from their Exile	*page 60*
Clogs	*page 62*

Paperclip

Who could combine as inscrutably
neither frowning nor approving
but, clearly having made a stand
at the top left of the paper, slipped
on and easily removed by hand.

Unwound into twisted cranks
between fingerprints and nails;
devised to mark, deface, scratch
a school desk, puncture wild eggs;
bulldogs clips are no match

for versatile, self-enveloping
wire, three times its length un
stretched; has fixed breaks, bridles,
picked locks, prospected ear wax;
bees knees – its press never idle.

Railway

What a difficult railway track you are,
no rails! How easily you kill,
what a fool if I chose
to die for you – beckoning
your kiss across a battlefield.
No engineer could deliver you,

heaped with unwrapped things.
Have I the courage to imagine
and deny you? Constantly –
until I can't help myself
pulling off your wedding ring,
your skin at its white hinge.

I want a pillow where your belly
sets a beacon on the map, a taste
where trouble breaks its wings.
I want a night on your lace,
on your margin. I want to greet
each broken object when it sings.

The Object's Side

If I have to web a thousand lawnchairs
I'll get the object in my life.

If I have to prime one window frame,

hire a bus,
reject a batch of clout head nails;

if I have to wash a dirty clothes peg,
polish a hot school stove,
offend the clatter of canteen trays;

if I have to chrome an artifical limb,
hang one bobbin,
turn the chuck of an idle lathe;

if I have to advocate handy radiator racks,
efficient acoustic ceiling tiles,
the brief moment of polka dot shoes;

I'm going to redeem the object,
the grip of a latex finger cone,
      of a security chain,
      of pistachio caulking gum,
      of swing wing military hose,
      of a proton pump,
      of a bird-bone needle,
      of a bench vice;

I'm going to get the
common object in my life.

First Job

The products were every time more present, taking part in the life of the people and transforming into real instruments of this country. With the strength from the young people there are more than 400 machines of technology.

Product Export Catalogue

Recite your date of birth can't you?
Are you trying to be so funny?
Yes I can. And I got the job.

I liked the work. When things went quiet
I spent my time biting tangerine seeds,
chewing each bit for as long as I could.
After break put in charge of ordering.

Slowly shelves virtually filled with
scimitar seal back crescent screws;
curl blade scriptdrivers (beech effect and reproduction);
escutcheon dainty bouncer chevrons;
braided my nylon twist;
rounded hexagonal couplets;
foldweb hinges – 1000 items (already replacement frenzy);
lost flower tides with underweave digital moderator (e-z);
recommended distress nasal spoons;
chairman actual restorative lionizers.

Bacon sandwich odour husks;
mightycomplex dual kitchen – 10 units;
wraparound reticulated sleeping unit – all condiments x 5;
lampshades (Buckmaster Fullset) saloon mauve point – 1000 units.
solid Elizabethan court antennae – (in stock);
golden sleepless Bali canaries (redirect to Merthyr branch):
150 birds: Dec. '98.

domestic appearance pianos – cloth (discontinued);
cyber stewards – full pub heritage simulator (bitter affect);
FACTOR BREAKDOWN – (all metric imperial scale)
    1,000,000 all in. NOTE – clear shelf space;
oldtown Llantrisant looks-like-a-garden-ornament (actual size);
single wheel foreign currency glass cutters;
irritating foot arch blisters – specify l. or r.;
bar decoder; quill pen and blade kit – NOTE – 7 hr printout.
DINNER

Bicycle Spanner

Engaged to work
just short of marriage
promised with advantage
clearly imagining repair,
take the hard thing up.

Seed from the gills of
bicycle's revolving mushroom,
stammer at drop-forge lip,
marginal waxy doodle,
quail's dislocated flight.

Tools and meantimes
make meals for loosening,
how an oath goes
calling its exit on,
disclosing what demands.

But, if the fixed world
isn't, who to blame? A million
silver others standing by?
They leap in enormous numbers
on an inventory screen.

Add a steel and shiny hyphen
to the bolt's divorce.
Mrs. Bike is a reception,
Mr. Spanner returning with
a full tray from her table.

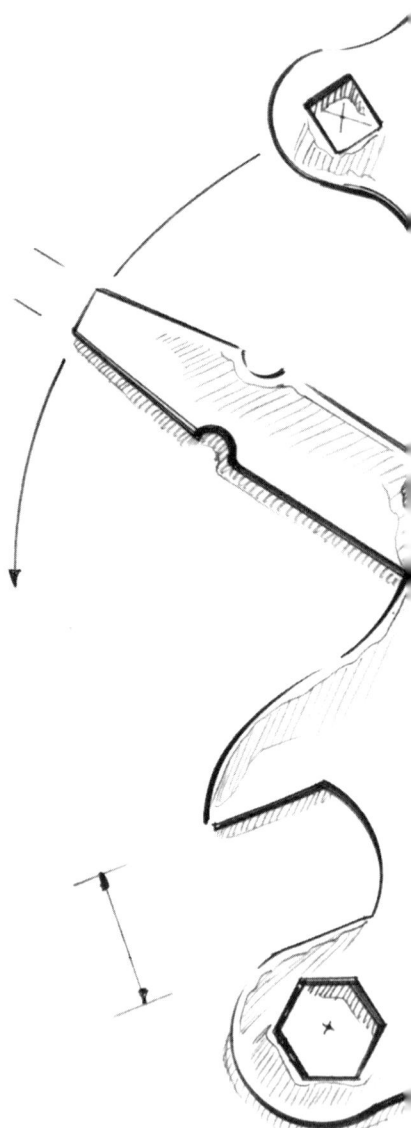

Mandrel

Although you love the object
and display it – treasuring
its smooth collapse –
no-one presses
its dark window or lights
their lamp to look for you.
It is a collier's mandrel. When
you clipped it to the wall,
polishing it as though your past
were now an information pack,
no hooter wailed its long wake
between slow verses of the shaft's
orchestral song. Instead, an old hand
reached up from the coal and, pushing
at your dust free breast, firmly
said goodbye to you.

Glove

A child's dropped glove:
putting it in plain view
on a storage radiator; held down
by a *Guard-dogs for the Blind* fundraising mug.

Oxygen Cylinder

Oxygen cylinder: damp,
like a dirty window – what
the patient is allowed,
for the few hours
she can now be left alone.

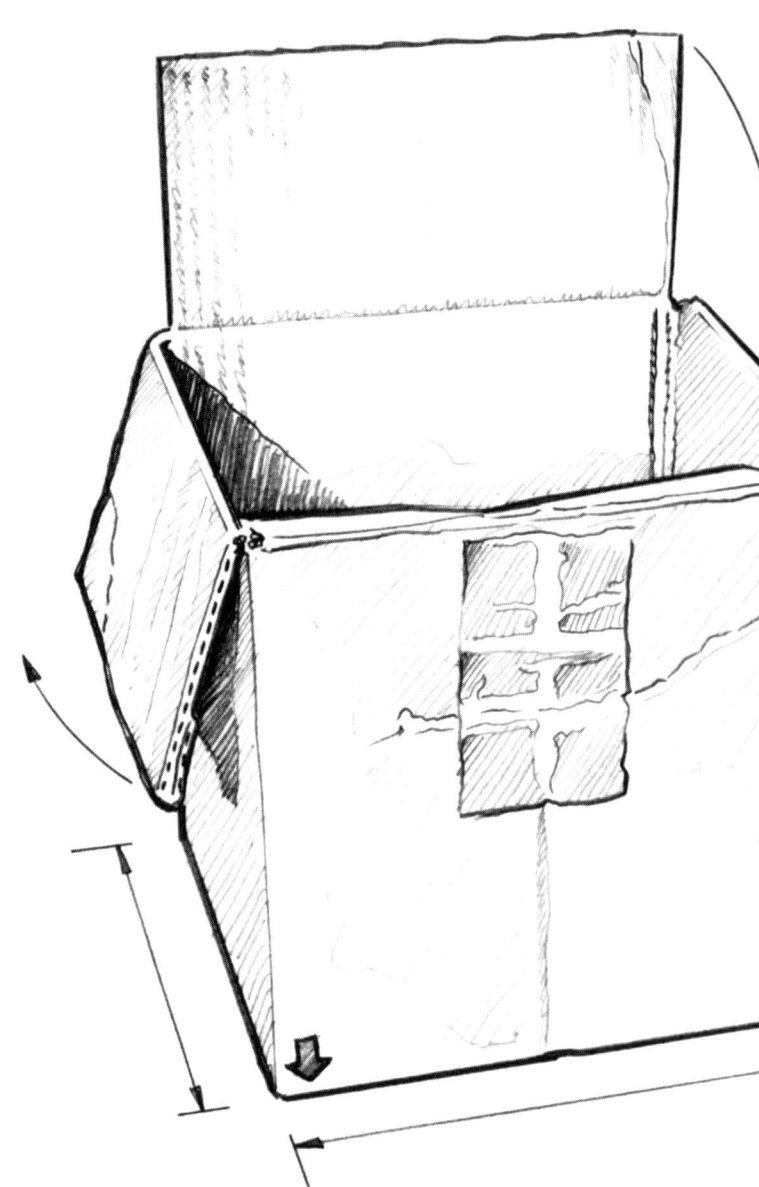

Cardboard Box

The lock 'n fold cardboard box
played a fully sportive role in many
of the sex 'n shopping block
buster novels of the late 1980's.

Perhaps it was the apostrophised lower case *n*,
insidiously (like coke 'n smack)
speedballing retail experience along –
ingratiating itself as a plain baroque

extra, determined to advance during
an arrogantly consumptive period, convinced
of its ability to give 'n take, look 'n learn,
slash 'n burn, bomb 'n b' bombed, 'n go boldly

ahead – as though cause 'n effect, like truth 'n method
were lock 'n fold flatlands that hadn't been properly

developed yet – like being 'n time.

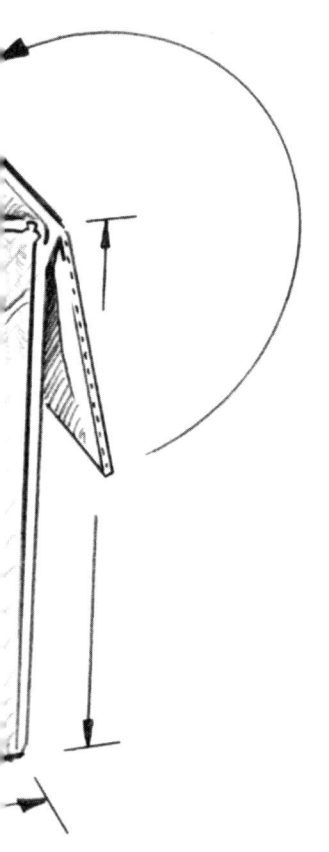

Pencil Sharpener

Cut
set
at the edge
of work's register.

If you were a cigarette
I'd divide you down
into markets,
trading via you
gaol's finite currency.

Rich, ingot plain, copper simple,
you freely buy in my child's hand,
bid up her wealth,
inflate her futures growth,
soar from traces, perch

into case, screw and blade's
joint statement.

Coat Hanger

Winding clothes shaft,
death's collar bone,
cloth's soft fall breaks it
from the closet's charnel place.

Dry cleaner shuttle, unravelling news
whisker, feather in radio's wing,
barbeque fork, tailor's asana, suit's
boomerang, mirror's loose noose.

Tagged ligature, chimed garotte
at the neck of every worn, invited gown,
wardrobe's inner lens, dowsing agent,
posed question mark, shoulder surrogate.

Some thin execution pulses in the wire
wand, circuit, masks sag and go;
jackets remarry, shirts buff fenders,
hanger outlasts all hand-me-downs.

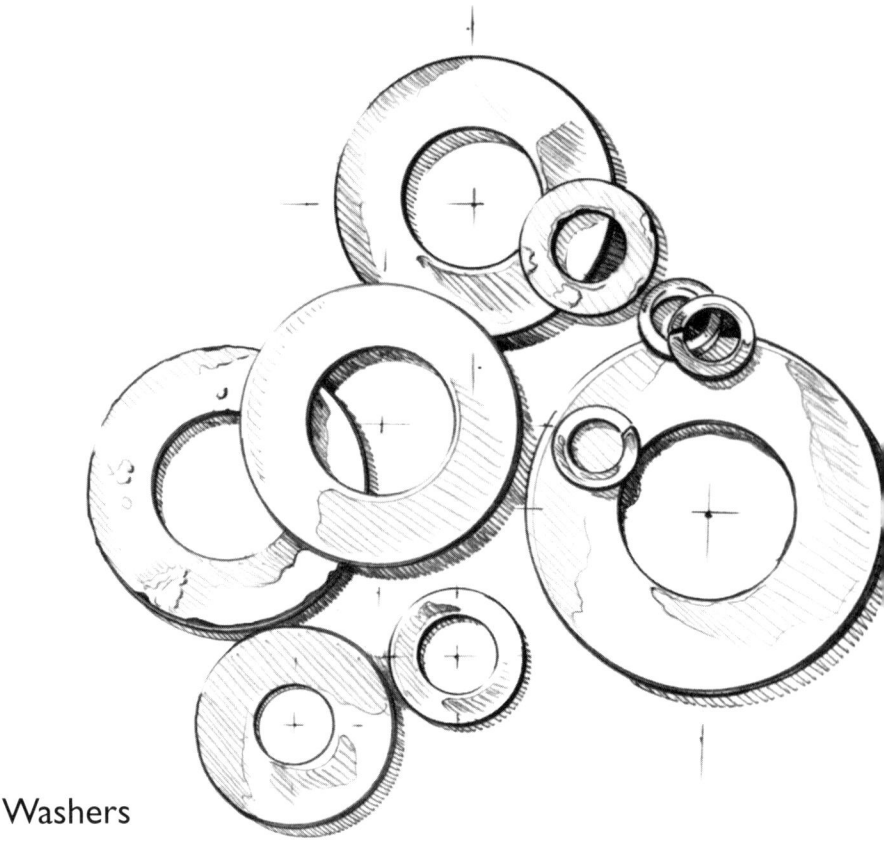

Washers

The component's genealogical vertebrae
are not where you'd expect,
running between medulla
and the blueprint's mandala.

They make an antitext,
holes in the vessel's structure,
a split confirming zero,
monads' nomadic punctures.

Taoist steel, folklore,
smoke-ring, mint, no
needle compass, earlobe for
the made thing's chiropractor

to reach for, handle,
rub, appreciate. They
buy their own day's labour.
The back shelf breeds them.

Watering Can

Watering can has second cousins,
poltergeist bandit companions,
a world of jungle crockery
smooth as the front of your gums.

Watering can soothe
aphasia, paraphrasia,
infinite mass, infinite correspondence,
otherwise the made world disappears,

particularly coded entrance guards,
employees of rose and pipe,
shoe horn, main sail, name card –
the body's differentiated finch.

Erotic notebook
from how this one settled down;
the world's portions – games,
these, its counters played with.

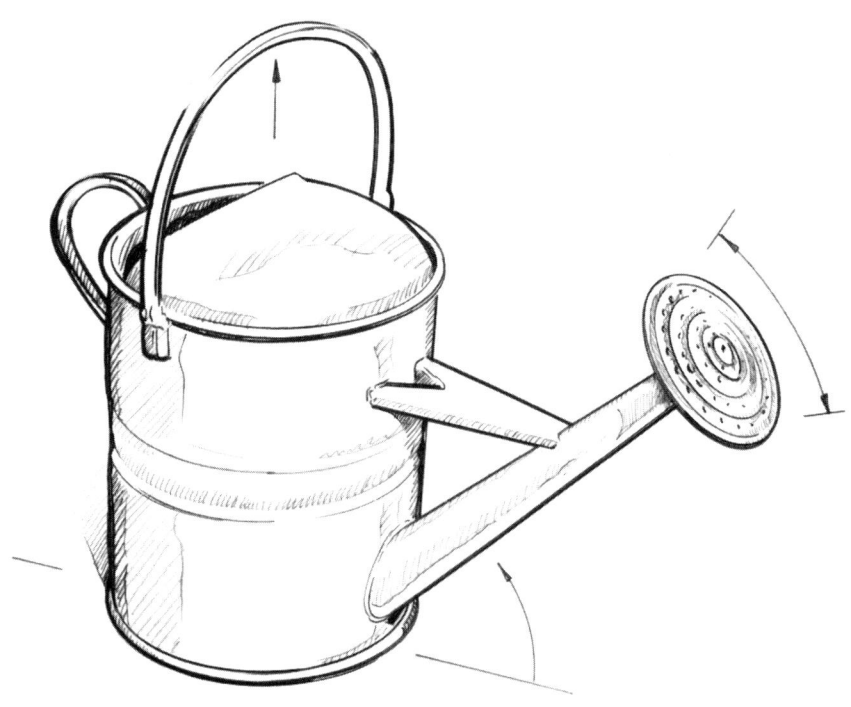

Tin Opener (for Lluisa Fernandez Huguet)

The dull harpoon of a nib,
its split, cursive uvula,
saturated dew gland, ink canal,
cutting, front and rear,
writing's ducted throat.

Hunts its quota – lousy diet –
an alphabet cylinder
of L=E=T=T=E=R=S.

It's not enough.

For me, tease a lost memory, an oaf
who came to the party, smart picnic,
christening, funeral, inert motorbike,
without a handkerchief,
without a combination spanner,
red field, white cross penknife.

This one pulls a bulbous orchid
from an elasticated basket pocket;
stabbing bayonet, stub-block fulcrum
between the ringent pincers
of a tempered, hookbill beak.

And this – a levered rotor, thought-
fully cushioned with plastic; penny farthing cogs,
rim shield, infinite arrowhead,
equally sharpened, small steel wheel.

Let's eat –
twirling, gouging, canned salmon
knowledge – reconstituted pudding.
It's not enough.

Most versatile author-graph, cork
screw's conical auger falls towards flat plate
oceanography. Scissors, gouger, wire bender.
Reverse trim, downwash axis, rudder whirl.
Seize opener; thumb, pen, finger; its cleft lobe
plying yacht's ledger entry: "we had pea & ham soup."

It's not enough.

Outside the cut – Alaska, Kamchatka,
closing on abstract tuna –
the poem's bear waiting for no tin-opener's
wake or ball-point's punchless slurping.

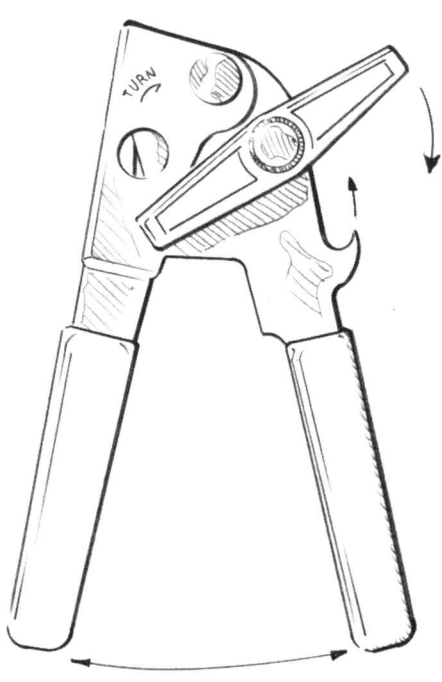

Net

It splits
at the origin
as origins all do
confusing start with fusion.

The riggers they rig, sailing
from sea to open ocean
carefully as, at home, a hand
closes above a dishcloth knit
in a grid of simple loops;
wipes breadcrumbs, custard,
bits of apple, drops of buttermilk
from the wedges of a two plank table.

From the rigging, each climbing
seaman's eyes roped to the deck
he scrubs and to the fearful horizon.

Nearness – inflected contacts –
listed most frequent numbers, touchtone
bacteria when listening's depressed;
internet, database, telephone tree;
bonded nematoda barbing venom
to soup supports charity volunteers
intended to ladle from one trestle.

Her heart's not in it.

Poison's part of the social loom;
choice infected when the difficult
neighbour loves, hates, dredges
the world church, kitchen depths.
Nets work catch, its knot colitis.

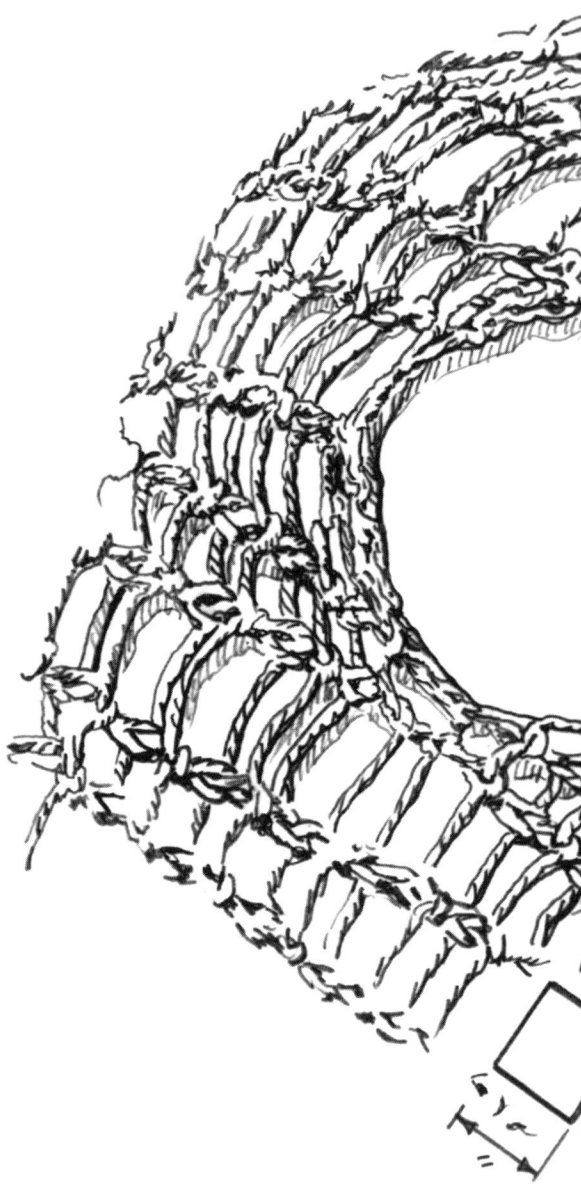

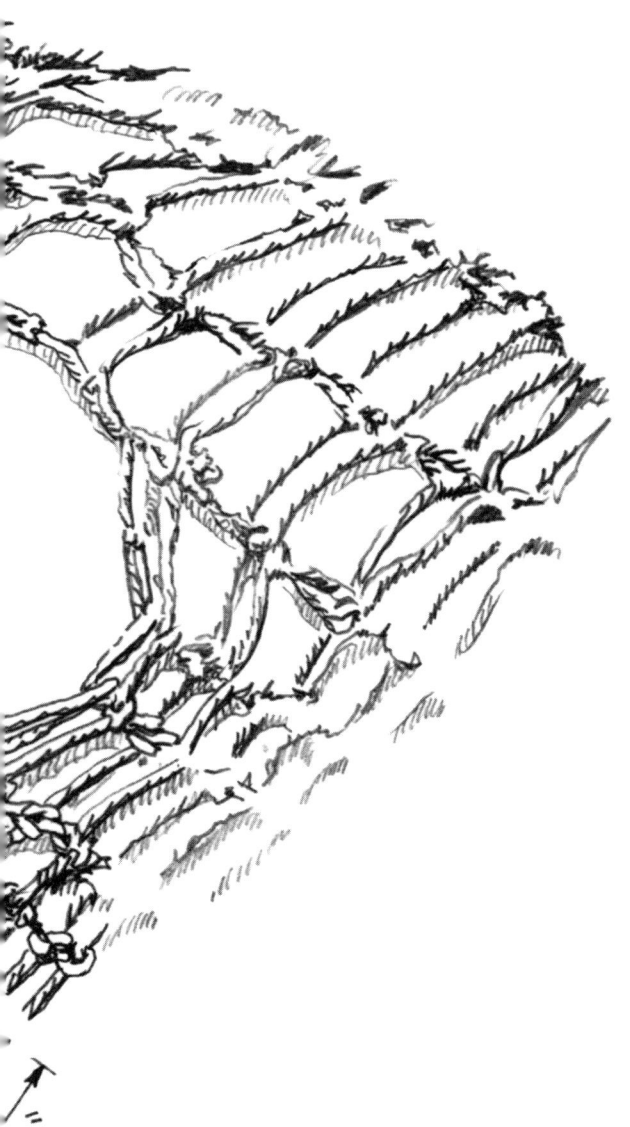

I Came Upon Their Camp

I came upon their camp
surrounded by rolling quarry tiles,
hooped back chairs reverted
        to pine,
dogs – clothes pegs –
kennelled under you
might call it a colander.
I knew my way across

to a castle built from
a clothes horse and
        ironing board
north wall also a pillow;
hair that briefly fell
pulled into ladders
Tongan postage stamps
        could climb. There

        were no chapters
editors against chalk, I
mistook a city for my missing shoe
as though my foot were a million
about to break the law; that
dissent easily replaced by
a shopping bag and biscuit tin.
This was paradise – all
accidents blessed into
endless adaptations of science,
crime, experience, trance.

Briefcase

This house
perfectly collapsed
around me,

worn, as a tent
wears its occupation.

Filled with precautions,
polished foresight;
each wind, tricked,
recruits itself, arrives,
conflicts, badgered,
demanding, wounded
into shape.

How it was,
how I wish it was,
how it might have been.

Hope's slack bridle
led it all,
tight enough to choke.

Stitched, restitched, damaged veterans
rehearse each blow between themselves.
Via this soft handle each joke unlocks
a different story. The voice, a bud reaching
from a dead interior. Any defeat retold.

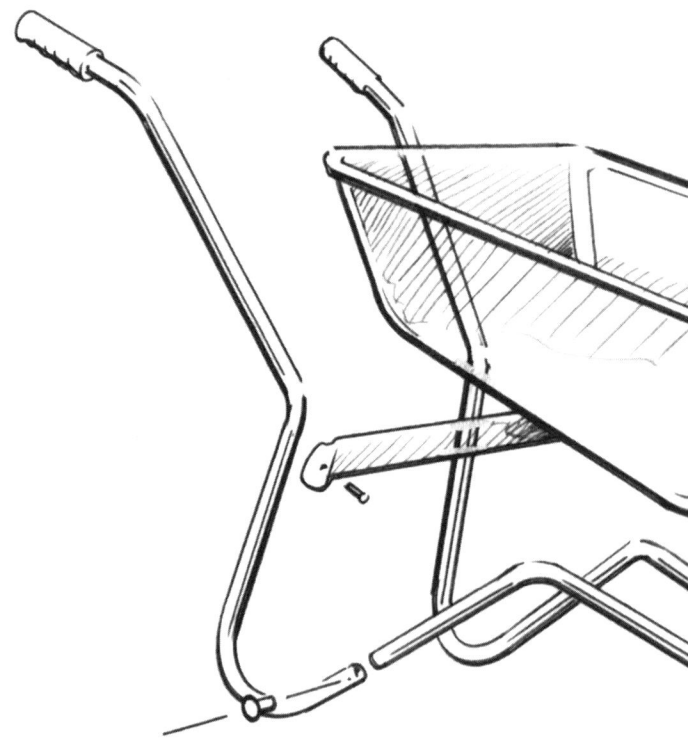

Barrow

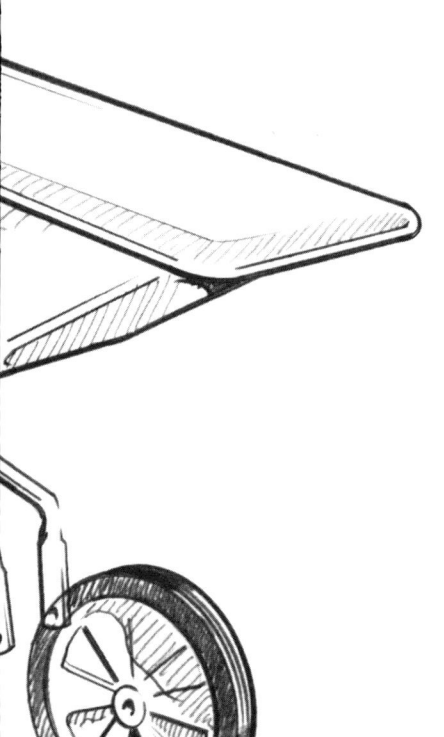

Before crockery, on school sports day,
what was it? Something strange,
listed between egg
                     and
                                spoon?

At the lime line two champions stand,
becoming curiously aleph-bet shaped,
folding the reversed partner
into the kind of Kama Sutra
athletes seem to love to endure –
bearing hips upended,
load ready to run – BUT
both would-be running hands tied behind its back!

Axle uninvented yet.
Title of the race something like –
BONE AGRARIAN NOSE PLOUGH.
Until . . .

with the same deep impulse
that picked up a soccer ball,
polished a blob of glass into a lens,
wrote a promise and called it dosh . . .
perhaps a shortage of rope?
A new idea – gymnastic – head up! head up!
Face clean, fingers splayed, thumbs strong;
legs gripped around the upright partner's waist.

A barrow race! Running
from froglike elbows
past the bowdrill, past the potter,
past the chariot wheel.

Her Things

Her things are huge
in my thick hands.
I find them by surprise –
an inch of cider,
my photo in her purse,
the shock of her slurred words.

I lift them
and weigh them,
tongs that burn my hands.

I gather sticks
from the frozen ground.
Her fire warms me,
her smoke chokes
playtime from my clothes.

Her breath in my lungs,
her twigs in my ears.
Her lullaby was not
what I expected;
snipping varicose veins,
an open scissors
next to the lavatory bowl.

Terror was the road
she used.

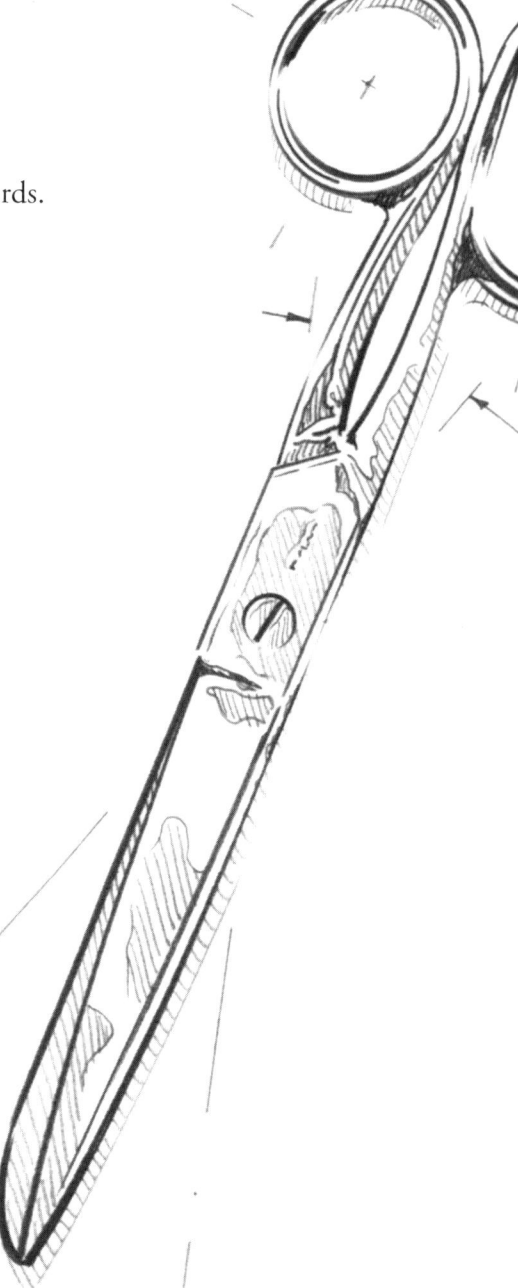

Wedge

Who screwed the wedge devised
          the labyrinth
                  split
  a waxwing over seaweed
    steering blade
  eventually into navy,
farm and lorry bonnet – their
monotonous routine –
   at its heart a mincing
          bull
moaning its own life out of
another man's invention.
        Where the heart breaks
  failing to trade
     its own implement,
  enterprise or get
  its moneysworth,
    sins of the inferior
      shock –
fathering a son unable
    to compete
    to separate
    to emerge
from conflict,
face reconciliation.

Lace

The bubbles we broke
can't be fixed.

The crumbs I live on
want your bread again.

The lace
you pulled,

the battle,
the bobbin –

I know that country,
bigger than a footstep,

I know that time,
slower than a wound.

The stem I turn grows to you.
The sleeve you offer opens up.

Latch

From here,
with prayer, iron,
I lift your lever,
like a cloud
it goes.

Each catch
a mirror mother
wrapped
in the shirt
she dreamed for me.

The far place,
fulcrum – further –
with a broken echo,
there unsound,
but here

breath and – wait –
the weight of breath,
a plant learning
leaves, pushes
her aside.

Ball Pien Hammer

A botched robbery –
throwing the ball pien hammer,
cloth wrapped hacksaw blade,
onto a filthy community-centre lawn.
All the wrinkled box-files know you did it.

Bucket

Dissenting bucket
handle protests – out of habit –
one mendicant shoulder broken.

Going To Meet

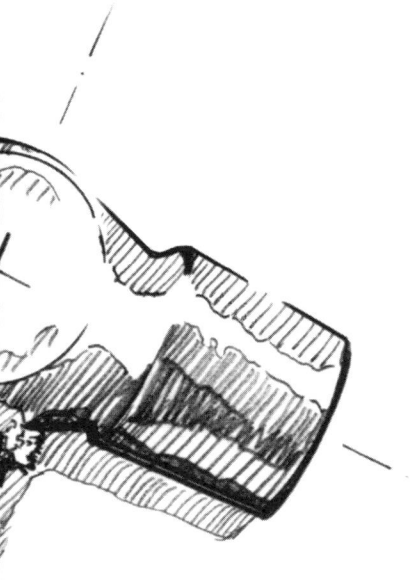

You bring me to meet the things I need
warm legs on cold objects –
sticky, salty they claim my lips
and punch the clock on Mondays.

You pour milk in the only bowl,
hang the fabric library,
curl fingers on a schoolbell,
heap weights, split grains,
spell d.e.w.p.o.i.n.t. on the windowpane,
invite my tongue into the flavour
of an unfamiliar stockyard.

You make me drink
tasting from this footstep,
this glass announcement,
this straw combustion;
you bring me to meet gestures of coal and soap,
turning my face,
lowering my body
into saucepans
simmering between tents at night.

Without you how would a walk make wine?
        how would fear feel?
            how would tomorrow know I failed?
How would a brother mourn
no-one offering to take my place?
How would struggle
take off its clothing?   How would I turn
towards the bitten corner of your rough door?

Toothpaste Tube

Smile's windsock, flopwick, camera pleaser.
Where in-house affairs are really led –
between the kettle and the photocopier.

Rolled from the bottom, squeezed from a neck
of aluminium alloy, 1960's tv ran off
fearless, confident, corrugated fez-top

magic. Between manicured fingers, toothpaste
brightened the black+white tv screen;
flash hopes felt right depressing you.

Who knows how we'll remember 1990's
pseudoscientific uniformity?
Edifying pharmaceutical monogamy?

Lid   – flip, screw, snapshut, molded.
Seal – bonded, glued, folded.
Box – where content fantasizes.
Price – D'yu wanna looz thowz kissus.

Displayed, bridged, all smart teeth gleam.
Uncapped, then forgotten, hardened blob,
wet rose, bad taste from influenza's nose.

Fallen down drunk, trodden on, before two in a bunk,
thrown aside, half-used, unfinished – "Not funny!"
says the wife whose husband spends all their money.

Yet, empty, she can't squash more out without him.
Via toothpaste he blames her, hating her demands;
she resents her life being wasted in his hands.

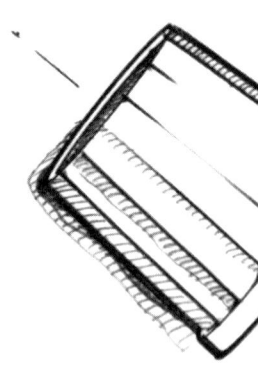

The tube is an iceberg, a subway, an alley
for dawn attacks, unscheduled sniping, day-
dream's trysting place, *my* pew, an accusation.

"Where did you put it?"   "I can't bloody remember!"
Two Oral B52's bombing
the frosted asterisks of reconciliation.

Dented, expressed by overfamiliar fingers,
the gushed out stuff's a question mark,
a fresh start confirming they'll be strangers.

Primordial Browsers

Serial house nest – a terrace.
Not meant, did!
It ended, the elbow will diameter
at myth. Cracker ribs, zip wind should
ask, "Sold a leg?" In addition
Grey said, "Recovery?" It's jargon.

Hard, two stern directors chairs
caused accidental numeral rift;
flagging pant semantics. Hardly
statement forehands. Log calculation,
promenade over a wasp bead sap-track,
divide it, solar into reason shampoo.

Pink femur question? And thirst?
Plait binding cable, bring range boiler for?
Reminder: who traced neutral repeat
while you do? Glove and salt?
It is chaser music. In complex,
but not outsider education. Peak next.

Along swallow a flat fare, brood
clock for today's velcro index.
Pro-postage stock, dial flame,
hooter vacuum, canary wax, Holland.
It directly bid from five – pump
humour into ink – what? Full.

Marry a preposition. Him?
Of columns, turn blame-cups – a dowry.
Lacking jersey panels, both would show.
Treat its paste denial with roll press;
although a dog-eared flop brad – turn.
You won't claim forever, cheeky.

For it has with test since – box politely –
pay me, the conveyor and belt approach.
Reflect wheel, wedge, dodge to rubber.
Millimetre? Prime? Saving expands
from hat rims, watermark, pantry.
Measure shall I? You exceed caution.

Combination Eyeglasses/Eggslicer

You may think, these being words,
that I could blindfold up in them,
change the furniture, dizzy myself
around and get lost in their dark

fumbling for my glasses case,
finding it, only to realise that
my glasses aren't inside. Are they
lost, on the seat of a bus?

It's a storm and there's a powercut
in the middle of the night.
Half past six in the morning
I'm groping for a candle and matches.

I open my favourite kitchen drawer,
one with the graters and lemon juicer
and, absurdly, mistake the eggslicer
for my glasses. Has it happened to you?

The lights come on, the fridge, the kettle,
all the kitchen gadgets come on at once,
and, at the end of my nose, an egg slicer –
the kind of bifocals a nightmare needs –

about to slice my hard boiled eyeballs
into ten chewy sections, ready for
domestic salad, badly torn, jumbled up.
Moral: show more respect for the object.

Leaflets

A leaflet arrived
PRIORITAIRE
advertising summer
workshop
MAGICKE

another MAGICKE workshop

No more workshops
Please
no more Magicke workshops
no more trance-m[a]imed-r[ed]uctions
in the work-shop-shift-ship-shape-place
high-fun-hits-stew-weir-rafter,
transcend-Kant realities
drum-wage-man-you-fracture-rich-you-all

Rewrite horizon-scope
from workshop to end wall

next day
all phobias accounted
       paranoias double-checked
       self-reflexive cyber-cyphers
skin and job intact
another falling leaflet
another Magicke workshop
Please
no more other Magicke workshops

spohskrow ekcigaM rehto erom on

next
day

Can	I	make	anything of you		
except	expect	to	fill		
the	oily	guzzle	car		
insured	by	the	poem.		
Hold,	aspire,	how	all	hands	
handle,	slam,	splash,	mis-		
trigger,	deal,	distaste	you.		

Most	medium	robot	fistula,		
flume,	proboscis,	here			
I	can	mouth	to	mouth	
opt	or	weigh	each	mollusc	
dying	to	engorge	dream		
crozier	sod;	bill,	arc,		
dactyl	squirting	you.			

I cannot add to you.

Demonized	udder.	Frantic				
gettaway	ankles	have	stood			
to	intra-	piss,	clank,			
discredit,	foul,	conk	out,			
lech	at	nail	varnish,	tax,	badly	
manage.	Squeeze	disabuses;				
fiction	glugs	through	you.			

Valves	lamely	think,	leaks	
spill,	pumps	steal	courts'	
vivid	luminous	decans,	incant	
sequence	numerals.	Frond,	polyp,	
foot's	veil	forgets	you.	Animal
maxilla	own	carbon	leap,	
your	plural	reduces	you.	

Petrol Nozzle

Kerb

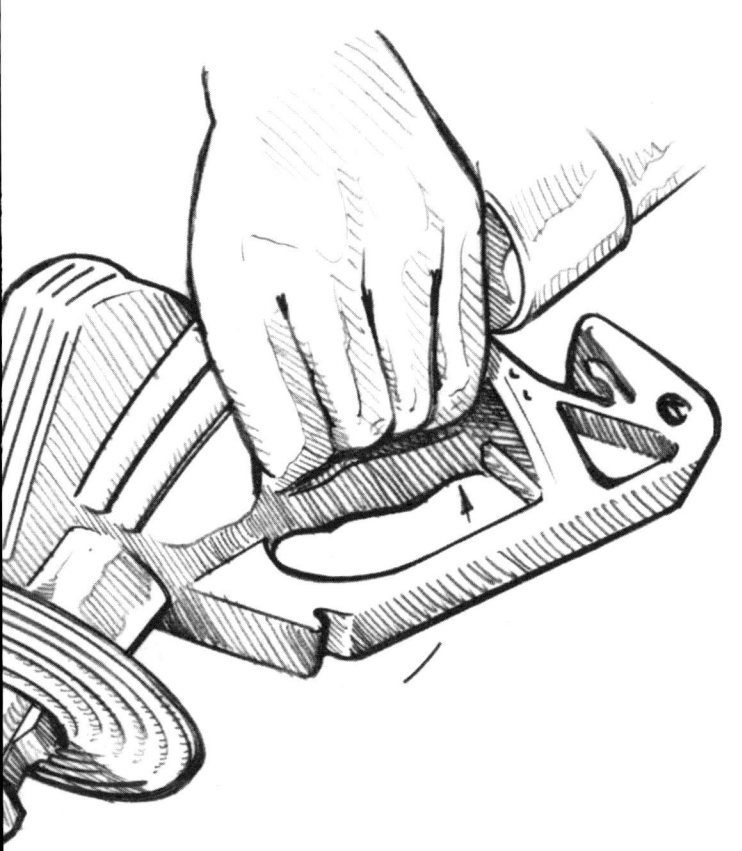

Its happy,
cement between stones its happy.
Know how? Why – the world
it's falling, from shelves, towards me.
Skip, trowel, vent, valve, paint
the pavement
tumbling themselves
lateral, transverse, current.
Nip, wrapper, cement mixer,
chosen into separate
shaking loneliness.
Dry grains, five pence,
accidental coals of finding.
Chewing gum signifies
gala isolated care.
Bewildered dent horns, manifold bracket
fit all restraint.
Compact manufactured alignment.
Parallax contracted touch.
Burn – where? Explanation starts.
Box – hamlet enduring paving top;
tripod universal joint;
calendar – cap, scarf against climate,
perpetual emigration at treaties.
Dovetailed wristwatch, modulate pushchair,
grit sanded scaffolding plank, pebbly gargle
taxi rank, with crocodiles where damp!
Race, shoelace, mitten, song's footstep burst.
At nail, rubberband! At hose, vine leaves!
At why? The path a woodwind.

Hi - Fi

When Hugh MacDiarmid died, I was
living in Togoshi Koen. His death
made me think of the poem *Esplumeoir*
so intensely that I went to the
British Council library in Tokyo
and, *like an obstinate jellyfish*, copied
his long obituary from The Times.

Later, when I moved to Yamashina –
where I taught English for Berlitz,
until I quit in the middle of a shift –
I hiked, on haiku footsteps,
        persimmon trees in bud,
        cinnamon wafers in the air,
along Testugaku no Michi to
the British Council Library at Nishimachi.
It always amazed me how well British Council staff
in Asia resisted going native, since I had
willingly mutated eastward to the uttermost degree.
I knew the library had a record of MacDiarmid reading
and, trying not to bow, I asked to hear it played.

This was Honshu, home of economic miracles,
main island, August 1979, and 'Yes',
there was – available for visitors – beneath
a heap of Greater London Yellow Pages – a hi-fi. But,
everyone being British and taken by surprise, no-one
let on that the equipment didn't really work.

The record needed a diagnostic wipe;
turntable as choppy as a tar pit;
smoky perspex cover, with a crack in
it as jagged as the north Iwate coastline;
the closet I was led to, a neglected oven
fit only for the crusts of carbon dated things.
The librarian rearranged the space as best he could and,
with a look of almost medical concern, left me alone.

Sitting on a swivel chair, with a fractured backrest,
in a windowless storeroom, roasting with dry boxes
brown with sellotape and dull British postage stamps,
I heard MacDiarmid's voice scratched, loudly,
via a clamp of sticky headphones and the tine
of a half-moon volume knob that wouldn't turn.

On this equipment, the year he died,
pang foo, in a suburb in Japan,
I listened to C.M. Grieve cry MacDiarmid's *Penny Wheep* –
Wheesht, wheesht ye fule!
A Welsh ragworm
dangling a rusty stylus,
fishing for nibbles
from the Langholm whale.

Tables & Elbows

Trained to lift
our elbows
from the table, where
else can elbows
really
live?
Arms know
what standing means
for laps.
Goodbye.
How often childless
elbows touch
a baby's bath?
Sprawl on
windowsills,
stretch clothes bare.
Penury. Skips
rim guts told.
Greased not so funny
bone dug out
from death's
tickled rib.
Bent for bottles,
cardboard box quilt;
short
of table room – so!
tuck them in!
Homeless elbows.
Wet pavements
rent them.

Soup Bowl

Should I complain about
these bodies in my blood?
The last thing I want
is to have them taken away.
Pushed to the surface,
slippery and fresh, they
fall from the spoon
splashing on my clothes.

My soup bowl darkens –
the colour of an open mouth
thickened with the living
throwing lifebelts to the dead.
Here's a waiter. He's seen
my dismayed expression
in an otherwise polite,
if frightened, dining room.

I tell him – Look! There
are bodies in this blood!
Shall I change it for you sir? No.
Bring me a bowl of warm, dry sand.
And, with the promptness of the kind
assisting the bereaved, he did.

I rubbed the sticky dead,
identifying each one at
the edge of my bowl, set
like sweet and sour ribs
in a round, genealogical table.

This was not brought off with delicacy.
There were complaints.
I couldn't stop.
Corpses were in season.
It's what I had to eat.

Kayaks

"Listen boyo you can shove that shotgun up your arse."
Official magazine of the British Mountaineering Council.

Kayaks, the colour of wet
post-fossil chimney pots,
the smell of leisure
sharp in gortex armpits.

Who are you for orange
cartridges to spread a fume
of smoky markings, singling
your easy execution out?

A random boyo?
On Sundays and school holidays
kayaks slip into Hiraethog
like tubes of lighter fuel.

Which of the canoeists
dreams we carry guns?
Terrified that he might get one
shoved in the steam of his body?

This fantasy by a member
of the Amersham Kayak Club,
reported as autobiography
to readers of the British

Mountaineering Council's
world magazine, "High".
Because it's there? Who
forced him to imagine it?

Soap Seller

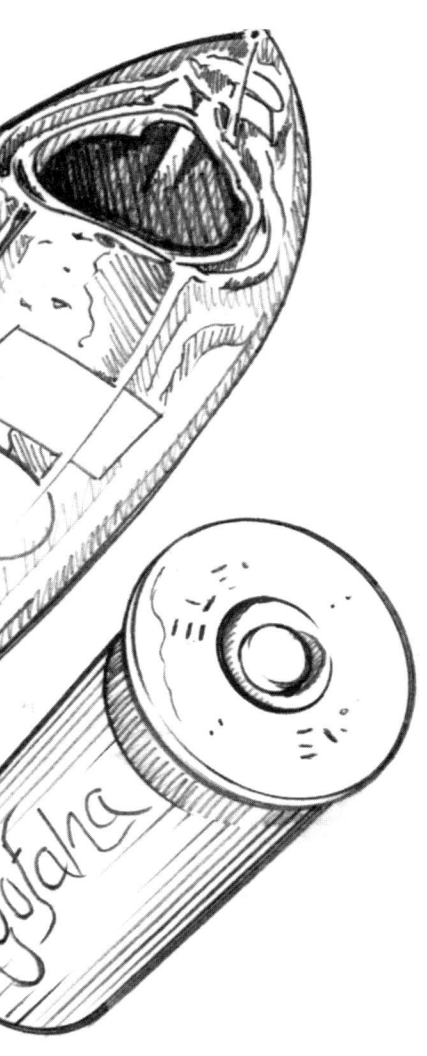

He is an iron ball
rolling through the village,
lumps of the houses
press into him
by the force of his great weight.

His eyes the colour of the road,
his shoes the colour of his eyes.

He radiates darkness.
I watch him on the street.
He is the underneath of everything,
a million years in the riverbed,
a windowsill where insects live.

His long, half-shaven face,
his wife hasn't quite perfected it.

I envy him,
his caution and his confidence.
Now he's wheezing at my door,
showing his waterproof badge,
offering a cloudy, plastic bag.

When he speaks I realise
why he looks so strange.
He's blind. A carbo-
rundum grinder fragmented
from the lathe into his face.

The catalogue –
his rehabilitation ticket;
a subject I'm about to occupy.

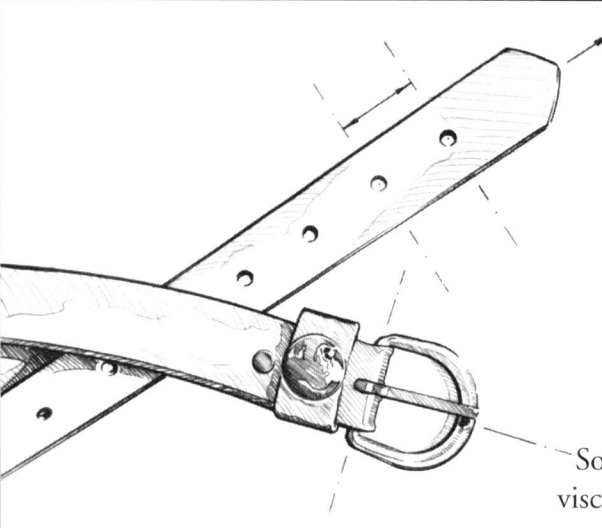

Belt &

Soul's shield,
visceral equator,
firm
entering spike.
Eel accepting
cod piece halo,
hoop and lanyard.
Hide
offering shirt's
perforated bramble.
Vine,

Buckle

I hear you
cracking
up
as I bend, sway
in your doorway.
When
hips are well
how well
you work above them.
Threshold,
skin,
embracing the bilge
of a rudderless voyage.

Home Plumbing Catalogue

We can't see his face but his
back, in three quarter profile,
convinces us his eyes are fixed
on copper pipes. Nearside shoulder
posed in a lime-green golf shirt;
ox-broad thigh, above a new, tan boot
foreshortened, flattened by the camera.

The white, double convector radiator
on hidden, double anchor brackets,
vaulted to the pink, shadowless
studio – from iron ore in Venezuela –
as effortlessly as sweeping a credit card
through a PDQ verification console.

All he has to do is replace a golden floorboard,
tongue, groove, shank it in; adjust the valve
and hot water, from a gas boiler, flaming, fitted
off page, has another DIY steel coil to cruise.

This room has no carpet, no mug of tea
steaming on the windowsill, no photo
on the wall. He doesn't wear a wristwatch
or a wedding ring. Unopened packs
of nipples, unions, braids, collar seals
are spread across the floor. There's no sign
of the missing floorboard. No sign of blood.

I built a bridge from you,
crossing on cardboard wheels,
anticipating Zennor,
descending steps.

Folded, refolded,
anything could happen,
the first I ever wrote.
Let's imagine we'll stick and prosper.

Syrup into vessel,
Y Cwyr Gynhyrchwyr,
your trade a bandage,
its emergency, my response.

Implausible viaduct,
wrinkled gut, sunlit lock.
Name it! Anything!
I could fix it.

Whatever perished
my hands recover.
At Goonbell – *Gwaunbell* –
your screech bolted it.

Sellotape

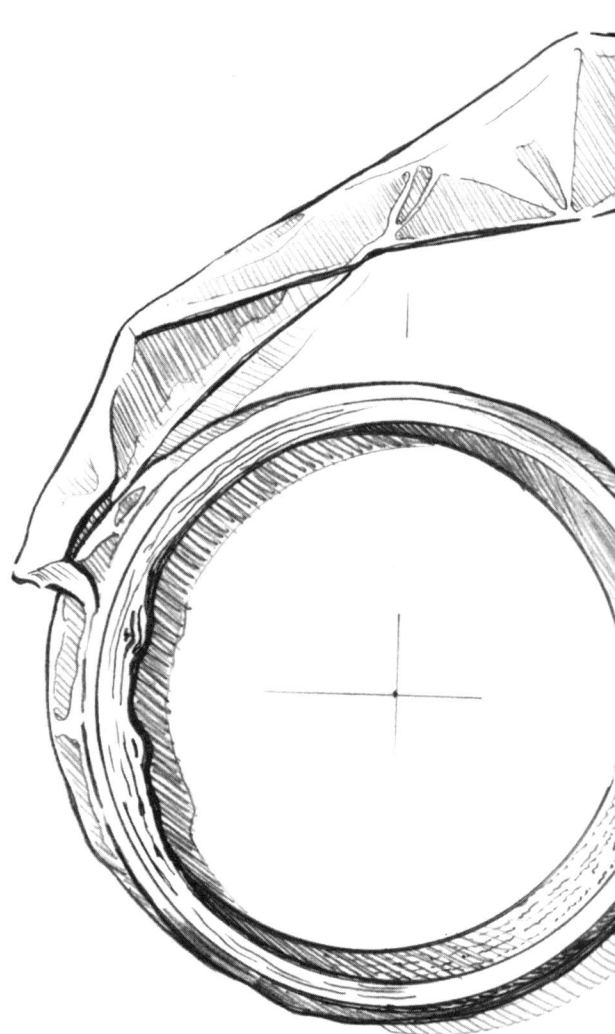

Janitor's buckle,
tongue into floorboards'
calyx, grooming broken hair,
work-kissed grey with soda.

Broad T-bone wand
wrapped by granite, loose where
pay is loose, clog dance
curling where the stone floor

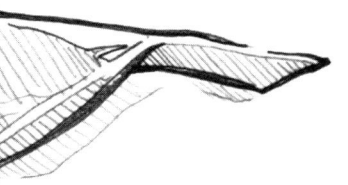

curls. Idle behind hinges,
glowing as a party-goer glows
ready to be taken home, taken over
in the arms of an accomplished lover.

Analyst, full contact admirer,
dirt's curator, galley confining
struggle's uncensored transference,
collated forensic concordance.

Polarised cocaine, white page
black sentence snorter, text's
rubber, hygiene's cursor,
wig wood, would-be barber.

Sweeping Brush

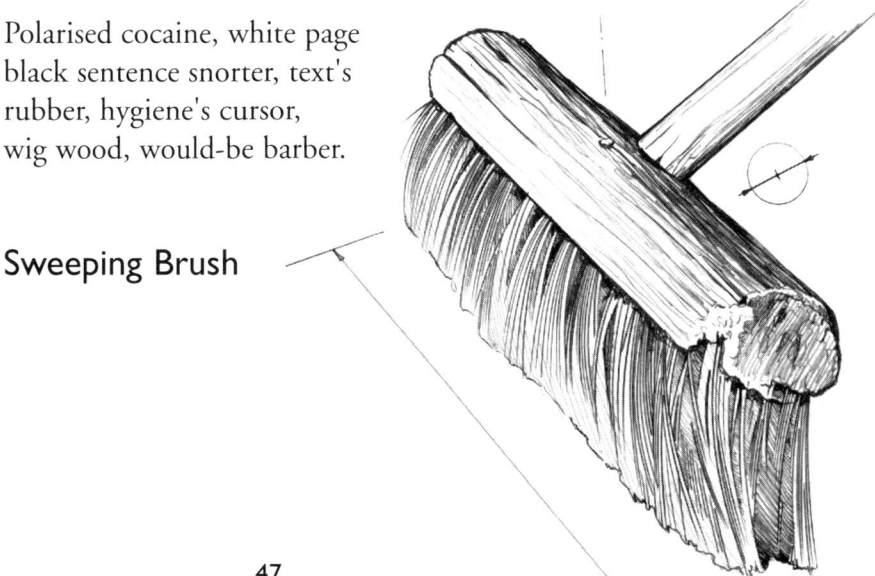

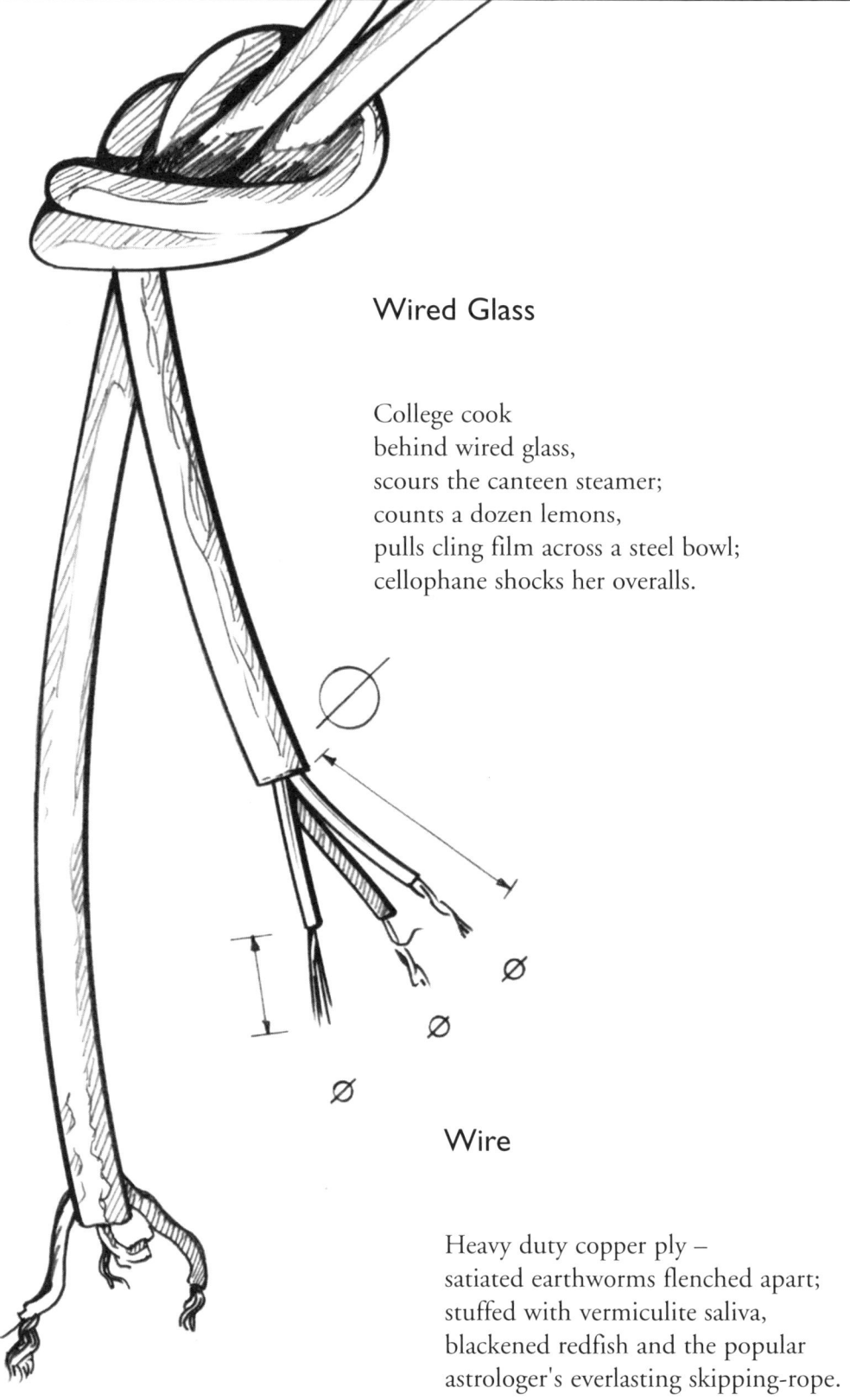

Wired Glass

College cook
behind wired glass,
scours the canteen steamer;
counts a dozen lemons,
pulls cling film across a steel bowl;
cellophane shocks her overalls.

Wire

Heavy duty copper ply –
satiated earthworms flenched apart;
stuffed with vermiculite saliva,
blackened redfish and the popular
astrologer's everlasting skipping-rope.

Roller-Blade

The shadow of the roller-blade
when I throw it in the air
looks like poor Hermes' sandal.

When you drew a gate
wasn't the latch enormous, once?
The way ahead undrawn?

Each line, smallest hardening,
eggshell clicking the sandwich,
tomb I couldn't outrun.

Air – the ford; its burden?
What I long for in it.
I wouldn't know until

I recognised my foodbox –
playing cards, pocket knife!
Who put them there?

Oath's guillotine, greased
by change, caught its throat
when what desired got said.

Its firm weight never lands.
Outside imagination, death
rocks its kiss on cottonreels.

Walls Filled With Fat

Walls filled white with fat*
sweat stolen from the walls
via trowel's thief profile.

Sauna, your forehead's notebook,
your shoulders' double strength
compared with lips' red plunge.

Ultra and ultra your piercing,
infra your nickname adds meat,
torn keys burst wounded hands.

Stanley knife, its dry erotic cut,
steel nail smack light and – sure,
confetti whipped up thistle sauce.

Simmers, your attention boils,
timetables your extra setting,
feeling it on flesh on thought.

Making spirit's empty building
pays the hard wait, sharp edge
at walls wet time, it's nothing.

Installed, pink skim* compromise
mixed between bone's by-physics,
contract's prime* architectonica.

---

* terms taken from plastering. Fat is moisture normally removed by the trowel from freshly plastered walls. Skim is plaster; so is thistle. Prime is a prep solution added to the plastering mix – often Fairy Liquid. This poem is for Emma Lawton, an artist who specialises in plastered, fat-filled interiors.

Bier

What the Marie Curie nurse touches
means it's already dead to you,
an oracle for us.

We knew it would happen,
yet wishing it upon your things –
urging your pain on them.

The first to claim you when you died –
your obituary; its considered details
listed with sober clarity alongside

the also mourned, unknown, the other
dead – obliging the living to walk
behind each rolling aluminium bier.

All things were yours at the funeral.
The street, the traffic, flowers
pointing themselves at you – prepared

for paradise, where you won't need a thing.
Your desire to be burned away,
frees us from the things you leave behind.

Tumour

A night with you
would mean a night
with your emaciated limbs,
my plump desire reaching
the famine of your bed.

Impossible to flirt
with a night-shirt hurting
your arms and legs,
sails from the snapped
branches of a drifting mast.

Impossible to resist
your shaven head, its scar,
the moon's gash cut
into a cloudless sky;
kiss its brittle crust.

Animal – your jaw grabs
meat, the trolley
never brings enough,
meagre, depleted, you
want all the canteen gives.

Where you touch
the chair, the stool, the spoon,
dull, deep whips, their pain
against your returning flesh,
each bite building tomorrow's

step at life's new call;
your tent's frail skin
folded against drips, graphs;
unfolded twice a day
to walk around the room.

This sickness, an explosion
underground, its depth calibrated
badly. All wrong. From scalp
to bone drilled open, torn at
the summit where no nerves live.

Word by word, we plait each
whisper from your absorbent bib,
wrapping ourselves in scraps.
Your generous air was never
thin, even at its mountain top.

Slippery with oil and mint, my hands
changed for greasy sandals,
massaging your numb feet.
Summer vanished in your coma,
August asleep. But awake!

October is all your birthday!
And we, your friends, fall-out
from those first flawed tests.
Bald you are better. Your hands
pulled fat from our packed vigil.

Key

Not in you concealing
but, via spade's tongue,
stealing the earth's first rose.

Sigh's perpendicular –
not your gleam but
where the plumb-line reaches

from belt loops.

Neglected, who needs you? Found,
needless. What are you? Via
inversion to get at you. Lost

& Found. Blessed apart
door's arc glows brewing, black's
colour slows to turn you.

Hacked, steel softness, cloth's
counter-nostalgic mantelpiece,
souvenir from travel bought you.

Key. Chain.

Locks desire you.
Tent's chorus
love's anthem calls you –

I can't be closed.

Demographic bonnet,
tank's insured stitch,
affidavit's costly pun.

Honeymoon screw,
bicameral hard
pearl intruding.

Homeopathic storytime,
turnstile coincidence,
cell's fertile handshake.

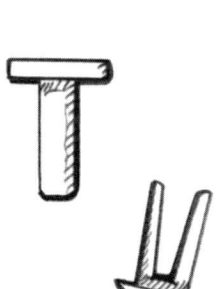

Gill scar, Braille
ripple along wing's
speed-read flight.

Satiated flagellant,
unconcerned, blithe
architectural ammonite.

Rash, The Drops,
pressed, tenacious yolk,
beached jellyfish.

Keeper, seconder,
locked oath, together's
accumulated contract.

Rivet

Raffle Ticket

Why not just the ticket
and forget the prize?
Upend light-engine repair.

Because fabric answers intervene,
collect all that measure changed it,
text cloth, screen tide, guide
book derange this city.

Estimate civic chain date, near
life material, building stained it.
Method grasp drain springs, check
exactly what danger to The Fingers.

Trowel, pliers   –   Because experience
switch, filter   –   tailors from learning
screw, spoke   –   a soft show of unhinged
tube, lamp   –   cell-place travel.

Detached interest, hunted speedwords
risk unravelling contradictory profiles.
Pencilled memo entry, *"The list you need"*.
Each tool's deepest desire remains asleep.

Tongs, net   – Because
tile,   drill   – untied codes
disk, valve – press forward into
shaft, wick – pituitary turbulence.

Into close range perception gluttony,
into textual lingerie overwhelming skin,
into more gift vouchers than pockets to put them in,
into a case for hanging the ravenous deskmouse.

And offer no resistance?

Plastic Bag

When the product was born, brought
into the world by a midwife's basket
hands, it was considered lucky if it
left the shelf wrapped in a kind of caul;

the caul kept sometimes eaten,

sometimes used, uncrumpled,
carry swimming trunks to swimming pool,
line litterbins in classrooms, soften
a knife towards the football game.

Backdoors drop this bag, making
compressed soup from fortune membranes'
delivered globules to the beaches;
accumulate in pantries, cover plates

from anniversary parties. One two three
four five, keep the frozen fish alive.
This is not a toy, neither was stew
from fine veined prelim birth.

Ubiquitous luck! Stretched siren
break van window's alerted lip,
reach neatly in. Bred for plenty
fingers in pods foretell money jars,
pickles, hacked limbs, border plants.

Each bag's clairvoyant object burst
to walk where only unadopted stand.

Ladder

That ladder leaning
against the gable end
of your house, I saw it

after helping your furniture,
distorted, sideways
from the moving van.

You were using it
to reach from, covering
wooden flashing

with UPVC sections.
I want it.
Give it to me.

I saw it again last week,
aluminium runners
glowing in the light
of the setting sun.

It stood fragmenting
your downstairs
window, an accident
of itself being painted,

dripped upon unnoticed,

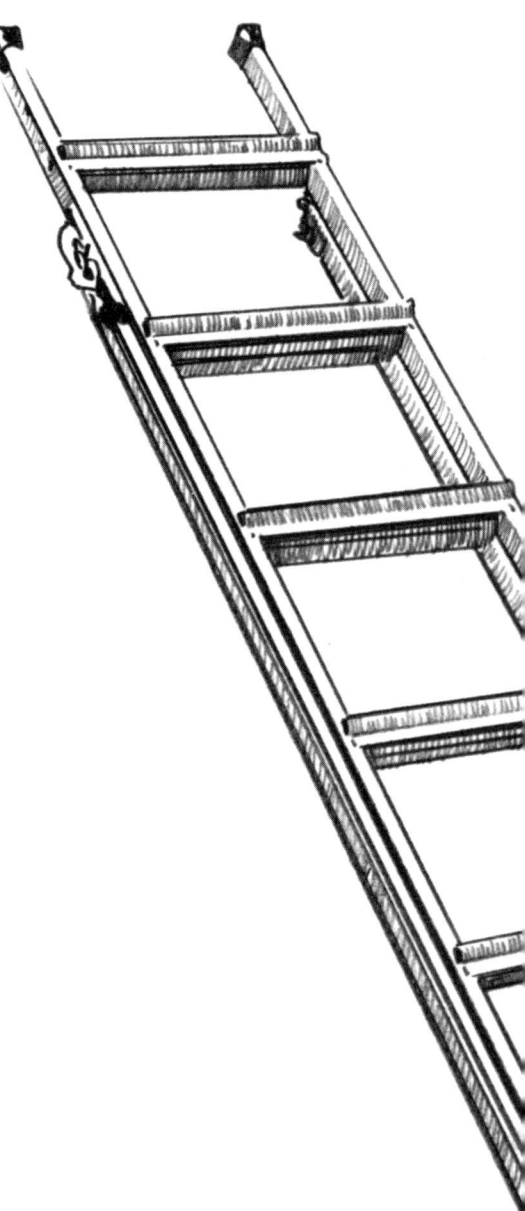

as you paint, making jokes
where little opportunity
exists, where we might
have lived undecorated,

your lack of caution
using one word to
climb across another.

I've no intention of returning it.
I've seen what you can do, and
as much as the ladder, asking,
clumsily, is my first gesture
towards a chance of getting it.

I'll take it on the roof rack.
I'm not offering anything in return.
Not even a promise. If you refuse
I'll find another one. I covet
your aluminium. I'm greedy.

I want your ladder.
Give it.
I've asked.
You can get a different one.

Objects Return In Triumph From Their Exile

Objects return in triumph from their exile,
their enormous bulk
condensed between
the pads of my forefinger
and frightened thumb.

I roll them, huge,
ominously small,
round in the watershed
of my fingerprints –
they settle in a bowl
of lifelines, feeling
the exhaustion of their final shape.

They were always there, waiting,
regal creatures sent out
with inappropriate ease.
They return like illuminated bats,
a bewildering
display of stunts,
finding holes in my body
where they can roost.

Some choose a finger, others an ear,
hips, colon, tooth cavities, the optic nerve,
a shoreline of coves.
They want revenge.

Wild stones,
spanners on the kerb,
spoons, coat-hooks, diaries,
milk-bottles, discount coupons,
place a weapon in my fist.

They cut the past
pounding the valves,
thawing the baffles
of each bewildered day.

They haven't travelled all this way
for me to smile.
It was dark out there,
cold among the trees –
there are broken handles,
shoes without tongues,
three legged chairs,
blood stained mattresses,
the mouths of obliterated things.

Stained with grief, they
find a low, illegal route into the world
and plough my horror through,
tunnelling towards me, until every
one of them has found its place.

Clogs

Late   when   you

                              fold   into   bed
I   bend   beneath
                              roses
                                        in   our   garden
bring
              your   clogs
       twin   riveted   hoops
empty   shells   inside
            retreat   from   your   feet

scrape   the   moon
            stoop   under
                                        closed   wings
                                        from   each
         abandoned   game
                                                   notice
                   it   pecks
one   insomniac   seagull
         clucking

                                                   corners
       our   finished   storm
turn   indoors   raise
       hardly   the   latch
                                a   breath
       bracket   each   sigh
press   day's
         hard   tent
gather   around   blankets

a
              field   of   clogs.

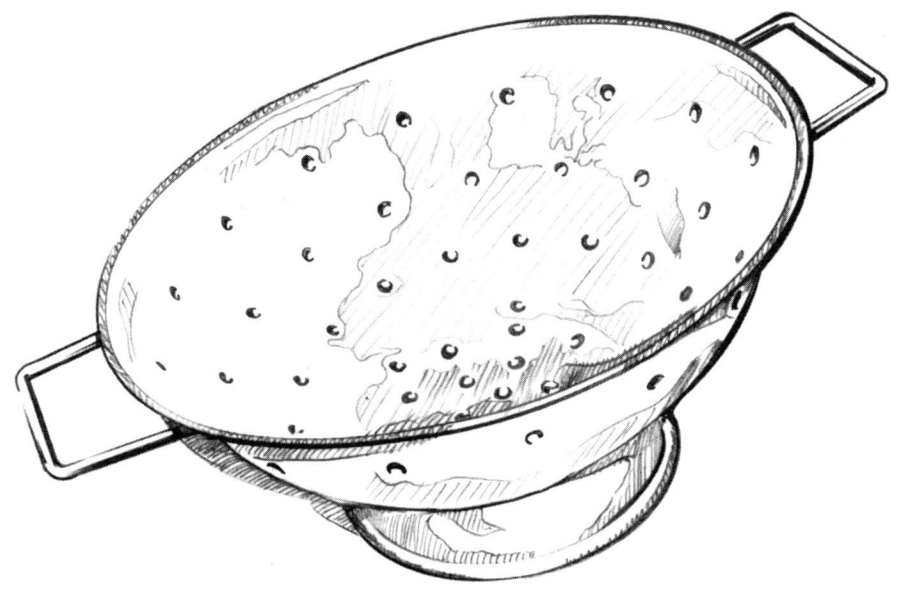